Nurture the Spirit of Your Humor

Luckner Pierre

authorHOUSE®

AuthorHouse™
1663 Liberty Drive, Suite 200
Bloomington, IN 47403
www.authorhouse.com
Phone: 1-800-839-8640

This book is a work of non-fiction. Unless otherwise noted, the author
and the publisher make no explicit guarantees as to the accuracy of
the information contained in this book and in some cases, names of
people and places have been altered to protect their privacy.

First published by AuthorHouse 6/10/2008

ISBN: 978-1-4343-8312-9 (sc)

Printed in the United States of America
Bloomington, Indiana

This book is printed on acid-free paper.

"If your sense of humor was required to work a job, instead of you nurturing it, it would learn to nurture you for the rest of your life. Nurturing the spirit of your humor gives meaning to your life."

-Luckner Pierre

Other Books by Luckner Pierre:

CHRISTIAN HIP HOP DYNASTY

A ROMANTIC SPIRIT: ENJOY
PASSION FOR FASHION

100-YARD FIELD GOAL: WHO THOUGHT
IT COULD BE POSSIBLE?

CPA WISDOM FOR ACCOUNTING STUDENTS

INVISIBLE ANGER MEETS DOMESTIC VIOLENCE

A LUCKY DOLL IN 3000

SHE'S A BARTENDER: IT'S HER BAR SALON

COMEDY LIFE STARRING LARRY DAWG

THE DESTINY OF POETRY: LIFE IN 3000

FROM BOSTON TO MIAMI: DEREK BASKETBALL

STREET WISDOM: LET'S TAKE IT
BACK TO THE 80'S AND 90'S

LIFE DEMANDS RESPECT

For more info, go to www.luck.com

After this Life

Album in stores February 2009

Films Written by Luckner Pierre:

BORN UNLOVED: YOU CAN STILL CHANGE
A COLLEGE HUSTLER
PAIN IS DYING TO GROW
RESPECT OR DIE
UNDER HER CONTROL
THE DANGER OF ANGER
LED OR MISLED
MY DYSFUNCTIONAL FAMILY
SCARE IN THE AIR
LIFE TURNS INTO POETRY
A RAPPER'S ACCOUNTANT
LIFE IN MIAMI
HUSTLER'S PARADISE
HAPPINESS HAS NO COST
BETTER THAN NOTHING
INNOCENT BEAUTY
HIP HOP DANCE
A ROMANTIC SPIRIT
COURAGE BECOMES YOU
TRUST NO FEAR
SPIRITUAL WISDOM
UNCONDITIONAL LOVE
LIFE IN 3000
RENEW YOUR FAITH
THE INNER MAN
A PROPHETIC SOUL

A WISE BABY

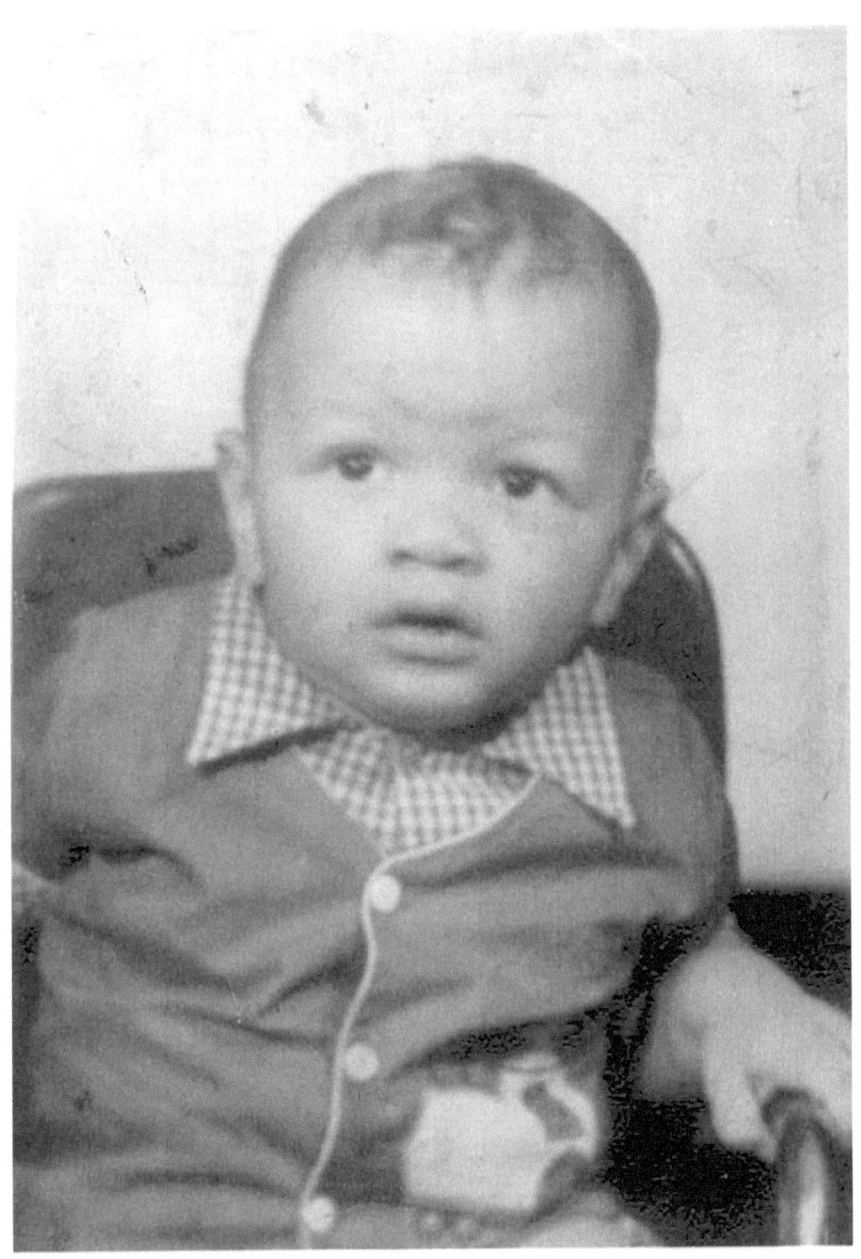

In Loving Memory of Yanick Meristal

H-HUMBLE

U-UNITY

M-MENTAL ATTITUDE

O-OPTIMISTIC

R-RECEPTIVE

W-Wise

I-Insight

S-Sensible

D-Discernment

O-Oracle

M-Maturity

Table of Contents

Dedicated to nurturing the
spirit of your humor

Acknowledgement

Sincerely, I first want to thank Sovereign God for allowing me to share my nurtured humor with the world on a spiritual level. This world really needs a nurtured humor. Without you, I would have no sense of humor. Thank you so much for allowing me to share my sense of humor that has been nurtured through your sense of humor. I want to thank my sister, brother and aunts for their support. I also want to thank Professor Fischer and Joan for your help.

I want to thank Lynn Martinez, Louis Aguierre and his co-workers of Deco Drive for keeping the humor of Miami Beach and South Miami alive. Fernando Brown, Patrick Eugene, Reggie Lambert, Aquil, Charles Moore, Sean Barnes, Leslie, Sherleen, Lonnie, Lumana, Oprah Winfrey, Les Brown, Cathy and Alridge, Alex St. Fleur, Ari, Paval, Nick, Barbara, Evens Milian and Abner Perodin, Carlos, DJ Irie and the Miami Heat dancers, Clara Stroude, Corey, Dr. Stein, Dr. Roura, Dr. Wainger, Edzel, Elsa, Emmanuel, Esther, France, Mark Charles, Mark Prince, Mark Timothy, Max Joseph, Melvin, Michael Harris, Francesca Febles, Harvey Ondriezek, Herbie Jospeh, Malcolm Gabriel and Mr. Linton (Stop Hunger), Hudson, Iona, James Lafaille, Jeff(a.k.a. Bless), Jennifer Cooper, Johnathan, Jonus,

Lance, Andre and Cedric, Midas, Mike Keron, Miguel, Mike Markland, Mike (FIU), Mirza Codic, Myrlchina (FIU), Nelson Aldomore, Oju, Orlando, Pascaal, Peggy (a.k.a. Arney), Bob and Weedan Sipion (Bible Boyz), Philip Jackson, Rosena, Rosie, Steve Gatson, Steve Bonnet, Ricardo, Claude, Christian Guerrier, Anthony Battles, Twin (a.k.a. Jermaine), Van, Will and Tony, Yolanda Gayo, Shikira Hayes and Kristi Armstrong for her beautiful sense of humor. I also want to thank all of you who believed in me. Thank you so much for the encouragement. If I forgot to mention anyone's name, please sincerely forgive me for forgetting. No one in this planet is perfect. In Christ, I love all of you. To God be the glory.

Introduction

My purpose in life is to write inspirational books to help encourage and motivate people to have the right vision for their aspirations. This is an excellent way for me to plant the seeds of encouragement, so the future generations are properly inspired with the right motivation for their aspirations.

Why I Wrote This Book?

After I had the proper inspiration with the right motivation, I had a vision of learning to nurture the spirit of my humor. I've learned painful experiences made me bitter and arrogant. To solve my painful experiences, I really needed to nurture the spirit of my humor because I could not find true happiness and joy from my own painful experiences.

When I saw how much I needed to develop and nurture my humor, it properly inspired me with the right motivation to write this book. It is a wonderful surprise to see myself write this book in one month.

When I think of a nurtured humor, I think of the sun because it activates vitamin D in your skin. Also, a nurtured humor gives you positive reinforcement and has a positive affect on others.

Writing this book encouraged me to find myself where I needed to be in my life and in the world and what I needed to become. It has given me humorous insights. In addition, it has spiritually enlightened and illuminated the light bulb in my mind. Even while writing this book, I had a burning desire for nurturing my humor. This book is the pathway to nurture the spirit of your humor. This book to personal and professional life describes powerful ways to nurture your humor. The goal is to nurture the spirit of your humor and maintain its maximum potential. If you don't nurture the spirit of your humor, you will lose the value of how much it's worth your life. Nurturing the spirit of your humor belongs to your mind, body and soul.

Back in high school, while in my English class, my English teacher made a joke that did not catch my attention. When that happened, he said to me, "You don't have a sense of humor." At that time, I did not know the true meaning of humor because I never studied the character of humor to develop and nurture my humor. Because I could not see the humor in any situation, I was unaware of the potential to develop of my humor that was hidden.

In addition, while still in college studying accounting, my sociology professor once told me in his office, "You first need to be happy with yourself before you can find yourself happy with someone else." At this point in my life, I was looking for a relationship even though the nature of my humor wasn't ready for one. Probably if I had good experiences in my life, I would've not lost the value of my humor. As I'm writing this introduction, I am convinced how important it is to nurture your sense of humor that can bring out the childlike humility and the best out of you. For example, when a baby is first born, it learns to cry. After a while, it learns to smile and laugh naturally. Now of course babies will continue to cry if they are not fed at the right time. However, once the baby is fed, humor becomes part of the spirit of the child naturally, so even babies learn to have a sense of humor. Similarly, when I take a look at the people who have had nurturing experiences, it humbles me to see how I could've been nurtured and trained to develop my sense of humor when I was a child. That is the reason why I have nurtured my sense of humor. I am so glad I found powerful ways to enjoy life with my nurtured humor.

Later on in my life, before I knew I had a sense of humor, people used to tell me that I'm funny. Even at that time, I didn't know I can nurture my humor to the maximum potential. After you read this book, you will look back and laugh at all the roadblocks and stumbling blocks that might've hindered you from success.

A nurtured humor is like the spiritual vitamins and minerals for your soul to enjoy life with laughter. Furthermore, after I enjoy my life with my nurtured humor, I want to look back and say to myself, "I enjoyed my life through a childlike humor." One of the ways to enjoy your life is to create successful memories for yourself and others. I find creating successful memories will pump your heart with a nurtured humor. As you laugh and reminisce on those days, you can pass those encouraging moments to your children and future family. In my family, no one laid down the foundation of a nurtured humor to help nurture my sense of humor.

This should be an awesome book to read. I will buy it for all my friends and relatives. You will learn how to nurture your humor even if it has been developed. Just always remember, without a nurtured humor, your humor will lose value. Nurturing your humor keeps all of your ages in new stages and is as important as the needs of humanity. Regardless of your age, you can nurture your humor. You can find humor out of a nurturing experience.

Most importantly, your sense of humor is an indicator to know whether or not you were nurtured when you were a child. The latest findings in this book will show you how to nurture your humor in every area of your life. Nurturing your humor is a sensible choice. If I had the chance and opportunity to create a college course about this book, I would teach it for the rest of my life. In addition, humor is a God's gift. When you can't take the stress or handle the pressures of life, what can free you from the agony? A nurtured humor. When your life gets complicated, you can rely on a nurtured humor. Nurturing your humor will connect all of your senses together. In fact, you will come back to your senses. Please read the personal mission statement that follows.

Personal Mission Statement:

To nurture the spirit of my humor to the maximum potential while I enjoy my life to the full

-Luckner Pierre

1. Separate Humor from Depression

"The main purpose of humor is to bring out the childlike humility."

"If you can maintain your childlike humility consistently, you will never lose your sense of humor."

"Understanding the exact nature, mechanism and dynamics of your life history helps you see where you need to nurture your humor."

"Nurturing the spirit of your humor allows you to experience a wise baby."

Chapter 1
Depression Abuses
Your Sense of Humor

Depression is an enemy to your sense of humor. I used to be depress a few times in my life, especially when my mother past away and when I had two deaths in my family. Believe it or not, if you don't have a tight grip on depression, it will take you on a roller coaster ride. If I had the power to go back in time, I would have had a tight grip on my depression. When I was depress, anger developed and was one of the symptoms of my depression. Then, it grew into a giant monster, and it took full control of my life. Trust me when I say this, depression stinks. It is like an odor that can never be put away unless you have a tight grip on it. It can affect your attitude and emotions.

What was holding me back from enjoying my sense of humor? When my depression found a way to be connected with anger, it poisoned my moral character. I couldn't make any friends; in fact, I didn't know how to make a good first impression. It was like I had nothing to offer. I felt I lost my touch with reality to some degree. Depression was the monkey on my back. In addition, it weakened my sense of humor.

Had I held on to the basic principles of Christianity and exercised my body more than usual, I would have felt much better and minimized the level of my depression. It almost costed me my life. At the time, the only thing I knew what to do was feel depress and get angry. I could not maintain my composure. As a result, I was not in the mood for humor. Almost every day I had mood swings. Depression hypnotized my mood to act unreal.

Depression is detrimental and dangerous to your environment. After depression bursts the bubble, people may never give you a chance to apologize because they may not understand the exact nature, mechanism and dynamics of depression. In fact, people usually consider your first impression your last impression. I myself do not agree with this, but it still doesn't change reality. Of course, people need to give you the benefit of the doubt. However, in reality, some people do not believe in second chances for you to present yourself professionally. In my case with depression, people did not find me down-to-earth because they had no way of knowing about my depression due to two deaths in my family. Even though it's their fault for not understanding the mechanism of depression, I still had to cope with their ignorance. When I learned the mechanism of my depression made people feel uncomfortable, it challenged me to learn how to laugh and smile. I just wish I had a proactive approach when I used to suffer from depression. Depression hurts everyone around you from your classmates to friends to your relationships in your family. Now, it is up to you to take and accept responsibility for your own depression. I never want anyone to feel depress; however, it will always be part of the human nature. After I learned the symptoms of depression, I prepared myself for any challenge that could come my way. The key to depression is to prepare yourself to study the exact nature, mechanism and dynamics of depression, so that no one holds a grudge against you. If you need to see a psychotherapist to help manage your depression, you will be on your way to take control of your depression. One of the best times to develop, sharpen, and nurture your sense of humor is when you are feeling depress. Please keep in mind only you would know whether you're depress or not. Take full control of your depression. With the help of nurturing your humor, you can do it.

On the other hand, the only positive thing about depression is it lets you know it is time to exercise your mind, heart, body and soul. I picked up this vibe when I went through depression. Even the therapist who I had seen told me that exercise helps minimize depression.

Equally important, depression became detrimental to the church. Even when I suffered from depression, members of the church were very concern and regarded me as a stranger because they did not understand the mechanism of depression. This happen because I used to have a history of anger due to the painful experiences I've had when I was a child. As I said before, anger is one of the symptoms of depression. Depression abused me so much that it suppressed my feelings, attitude, behavior and conscious. All of my potential smiles turned into unnatural smiles. Also, it suppressed my laugh when I would want to laugh and smile. I felt my ability to laugh and smile was shut down. I remember when I tried to socialize with my college classmates, but no one was interested in getting to know who I am. I just didn't know how to adapt to their lifestyle. At that time, I could not understand why my sense of humor was shallow. There were times I felt I was breathing to death as if a python snake was around my neck every morning. As a result, depression repressed and neutralized my progress.

Is Humor Health-Related?

Based on my experience with depression, humor can be health-related because the better your health the better your attitude and vice versa. For example, when depression took a hold of my life, my attitude was not positive. Despite the academic stress, I remember the impression and aggression my depression gave some people who could sense my well-being. I will never forget this experience since it taught me an important lesson about depression. Furthermore, depression is also health-related because it will affect the attitude of your health. Never let your emotions swallow your humor alive. Too many emotions can suffocate your sense of humor.

Domestic Violence Creates Depression

Equally important, women who fall in love with men who treat them badly are a situation that can turn into depression. Look at it through the eyes of humor, if you are in a relationship where your partner either keeps you depress or contributes to your depression, your partner is also responsible for the condition of your depression. Even though the law may not take the influence of depression into serious consideration, the fact of the matter is your partner either kept you depress indirectly or contributed to your depression in some way. Also keep in mind anger is one of the symptoms of depression. Therefore, depression can be created by domestic violence.

Be Alert for Depression

Since I experienced depression before, I will be ready to reduce it if it comes back at any given point. Let me tell you, depression is like a monster that keeps abusing you until you make the decision to minimize it with therapeutic techniques and methods, such as cardio exercise and weight lifting and maybe seeing a psychotherapist. Just keep in mind you cannot destroy depression because it is part of your human nature. After you study the symptoms and functions of depression and if you see any of them in your life, you should quickly attack the nature, mechanism and dynamics aggressively. You would save a lot of time for the pleasure of nurturing your humor. Nurturing your humor can help maintain an awareness of depression. After my depression faded away, it still affected my sense of humor. I then had to develop and nurture my humor, and it helped me recovered from depression. Through a nurtured humor, I regained my confidence. The invisible monkey was off my back. My depression was like a demon driving me crazy. Even after when I learn to manage my anger, depression was still hunting me. In addition, I later learned and realized I absorbed two emotional characters that used to be my role model. It corrupted my soul and contributed to my depression then interrupted the rhythm of my sleep at night.

Last but not least, if you have or had a death in your family, look for the humorous experiences because they will help reduce your depression. Also, nurturing your humor can reduce the pains and sorrows when there is a death in the family. If you allow discouragements, disappointments, disagreements, embarrassments and frustrations to get the best of you, especially for a long time, it will turn into depression. Your humor is greater than discouragements, disappointments and frustrations.

Until this day, nurturing the spirit of my humor is still a life-changing experience for me. Again, depression abuses your sense of humor. If professional help by a psychotherapist or therapist did not exist, I would have to develop a humorous depression. It would probably taste like a chocolate marshmallow.

2. Humor is a Natural Lifestyle

"A nurtured humor graduated from Heaven State University."

"Humor and humility can go hand in hand."

"Humor is sweet to my soul because my nurtured humor tastes like syrup."

"How healthy and strong is your humor at this point in your life?"

Chapter 2
Humor Fits a Healthy Lifestyle

Who is the most humorous person on earth? It shouldn't matter because everyone has the ability to nurture his or her humor. A nurtured humor can fit anyone who lives a healthy lifestyle. It doesn't matter who it is as long as that individual is healthy enough for good humor. A healthy lifestyle will help enrich all of your senses through a nurtured humor. Nurturing your humor is a heart-healthy choice. When you lose your train of thought for just a moment, just laugh at yourself. Nurturing my humor makes my heart feel like a new born baby.

Healthy Food is Part of Enjoying Life

The motto I want to use for this chapter is "The True Meaning Behind Healthy Food Is Part of Enjoying Life."

One time at a Barnes and Noble bookstore, my former college friend showed me a few words of wisdom in a book and then smiled and laughed with his humor. At that time, I could see his sense of humor through how much profound books he has read. He always had a sense of humor for reading books that he enjoyed reading. He was like a humorous anthropologist because of the way he liked studying humans. At one time, he told me, "Reading is simple, but it's a lot." I found humor out of this statement. Speaking of reading, I notice people, who don't like to read profound books, have not nurtured their humor. If people could nurture their humor, they will have an appetite for humorous insights to share with others.

At a pizza restaurant, I treated my former college friend for lunch. While we were eating, he mentioned, "Eating healthy food is part of enjoying life." From what I understood at the time, it means you can learn to enjoy your life while eating healthy food that brings out laughter. It made sense when he shared this inspirational thought. It was like he taught me how to eat the body of humor.

When you eat unhealthy food, you will start to feel uncomfortable because it doesn't promote good health within your body of humor. Also, it doesn't allow you to enjoy life to the full. Take a look at professional athletes. They enjoy drinking sport drinks during the game and eating healthy food during breakfast, lunch and dinner. Healthy food is part of their lifestyle. Then, it becomes fun and makes life funny to enjoy.

You should have an appetite for humor. You can train yourself to develop an appetite for humor. When you go to a party or social event, appetizers are usually on a table ready to serve each and every individual. While everyone tastes the appetizers, at this point a bit of taste starts to excite your desire for more. While this is happening, you have a smile on your face. A humorous smile is a great tool for building a friendship and invites people to come talk to you. You may end up having a friendship with another person who may have a great sense of humor.

Nurturing your humor has a delicious taste for your soul. I remember when I walked into an office. I saw a funny expression of words on a paper hanging on the wall. It stated, "Bang Your Head When You Feel Stress." It was funny to find the comical insight in these words to help reduce my stress. The funny expression of words started to release my tension and stress. Nurturing your humor preserves the quality of your life. Feed your humor with a healthy lifestyle. Spiritual food for your humor.

The Grapefruit Diet

What's so funny about the grapefruit diet? I nurtured my humor while I was on a strict grapefruit diet.

One day in the gym at a college, a student approached me about the grapefruit diet. He told me that the way to burn fat is to consume fat. In other words, fat burns fat. I then asked him, "How can you burn fat with fat?" He then said that the composition of the grapefruit diet is high in protein but low in carbohydrates. In the morning, I would eat two boiled eggs and drink one cup of grapefruit juice without sugar. In the afternoon, I would eat one pound of tilapia fish (you can eat any healthy kind of fish) and drink another cup of grapefruit juice. At night, I would eat vegetables with steak and drink another cup of grapefruit juice. For about two months, I would repeat the same procedure. After the two months, the grapefruit diet became soul food for my health. Of course everyone's body is different, but the grapefruit diet works effectively. Overall, the grapefruit diet should be able to work because it has an effective composition of what to eat at the right time.

Not too many people like grapefruit juice. However, what's more important-what your body needs or what tastes good?

After I applied the grapefruit diet, I lost about 30 pounds in two months with the help of playing basketball and weight training. In fact, without playing basketball and weight training, I still would've lost about 30 pounds due to the effective composition of the grapefruit diet. Your body must become accustomed to your nurtured humor while you continue to nurture your humor.

Duck Walks for Humor

Have you ever done duck walks before? When I was a teenager, I used to enjoy doing duck walks in my karate class. My former instructor would have my class do duck walks in a circle around the class. The benefit you gain from doing duck walks are: stronger legs, preparation for squat exercise and strengthen your calf muscles. When my brother was in my classes, he did not enjoy doing duck walks. However, I found it fun and beneficial for my legs to jump like a frog. Additionally, duck walks are very good for basketball players and for any sport that requires jumping and fast running. Besides, you should try it to strengthen your legs to prevent an injury from happening. The more you exercise your body and keep it in the best shape the less chance of any injury. At the end of the day, you will look like a basketball player with frog legs. Despite the amount of sweat, until this day, I still enjoy doing duck walks. Imagine if there was a duck walk dance. I could probably burn a pound a day. As long as duck walks can help improve my humor, it is part of nurturing the spirit of my humor.

AND 1 Basketball Developed My Humor

While I was still in college, I started watching AND 1 basketball, a professional streetball league, at around two o' clock in the morning when it shown on ESPN.

What does AND 1 mean to me? AND 1 helps develop and nurture my humor. Since summer 2003, I've been an ardent fan of AND 1. In fact, I love AND 1 basketball more than I love the NBA. During the summer time, some of the NBA players would play in the AND 1 game for the fun of it. It was just all about fun. The game of AND 1 basketball has a comical element that injects humor in the audience. For example, I've seen the 'Pharmacist' dribble the ball behind his back in front of an opponent player who tried to play defense. I just could not believe the ball was not stolen by the opponent player who defended him closely. When I saw how the AND 1 players maneuver the ball, it sustained my laughter throughout the whole time, and I laughed again when I arrived home. In addition, I remember when I met "Hot Sauce" in the mall. The experience was pleasant and fun. We spoke to each other. A year later, I met him again when I gave each player a basketball song on C.D. at the autograph stand where fans lineup to get an autograph. The song is dedicated to Antoine Howard aka "Flash."

Equally important, I've learned and noticed AND 1 basketball has something the NBA doesn't have. That is, AND 1 creates a long-lasting humor and freewill to create humorous moves with the ball. When I say freewill, I really mean the players can freely show their unique talent during the game. Despite the lack of rules in the game, it is still exciting and fun. In addition, while in practice playing basketball at Job Corps, the head coach said, "Basketball is supposed to be fun." When I heard this, I felt the motivation for the game of basketball. In fact, I think any sport you play is supposed to be fun. AND 1 basketball can be looked as compensation for the lack of rules. As soon as 'Hot Sauce' does a tricky move and gets the opponent player looking for the ball, the audience laughs at the opponent player. Even if 'Hot Sauce' misses the jump shot, you can still hear and feel the excitement and humor from the crowd. This is something you don't find in the NBA. On the other hand, I'm not saying the NBA doesn't inject humor in the crowd. The NBA has something AND 1 doesn't have. That is, the NBA carries and maintains organize basketball on the court. The NBA rules govern the players in the game.

Additionally, I was watching a short documentary about Tim Duncan, who plays basketball for the San Antonio Spurs. The part that struck me the most was when his coach learned Duncan has a sense of humor. It allowed Duncan and his coach to get along well, and they succeeded in the NBA Finals. This indicates how powerful humor can be through basketball.

In regards to AND 1 basketball, without the entertainment value of AND 1, it takes away the humor out of the basketball game. Humor is a special part of the entertainment value of AND 1 basketball. If you enjoy tricky moves, no-look passes, back-door plays, alley-oops and creative dunks in the NBA, you will definitely fall in love with AND 1basketball.

WAND1 League

Will there ever be a WAND 1 league? Possibly because nowadays we live in a woman's world. At one point, I thought about investing in this great idea. Hopefully, in the future I can make it happen.

On and Off the Street Court

Whenever I play basketball with a few guys I know, one of them plays with a personal approach. His basketball persona irritates my attention because he lets his ego control his persona on the court. However, when he sits down to rest, his persona goes back to a social approach.

Whether you're on or off the court, good humor can help you stabilize your mood to stay healthy at all times. You should want to study peoples' social life and personal life because we live in a world that accepts dark humor (sarcasm) but not good humor.

The World Accepts Dark Humor

Most people do not reveal their true identity because they develop the type of human being that they would like to be. They love what they do, and they do what they love. How you handle each area of your life reveals who you really are inside; also, because of the human nature, inside of every character there is a character flaw that wants to break the law. Dark humor affects your well-being as soon as good humor detects it. Equally important, dark humor is a sign of weakness to the individual and to the world. Since dark humor has already develop a dark and evil world that we live in, nothing good will ever come out of dark humor. Dark humor generates rumors that can affect your reputation for a long time. Good humor will never share the same space with dark humor. Validate the power of good humor to completely remove and erase dark humor. Therefore, trust good humor and have confidence to stay away from dark humor.

A Yellow Joke

While my humor was still folded in half, I met a young and very beautiful lady. Her humor shined like the sun. Even though her sense of humor caught my attention, I still wish my humor had the same radiance as her humor. For example, when I told her, "I can make one thousand dolls out of you," the way she laughed and smiled was encouraging to my heart. I saw the laughter in her eyes.

Because of her beautiful and shining humor, I would like to invent a remote control doll that looks like her, act like her, talk like her, and walk like her. I truly believe it would inject humor in most people. Also, it would be like keeping the flesh of this doll staying fresh.

Her sense of humor represented the beauty of the sun. Unfortunately, because my humor was still folded in half, we could not connect on a spiritual level. When I look back at those days, I clearly understand why everything happened the way it did. At the time, my college life was missing a nurtured humor. If I could go back and change one thing, I would nurture my humor each and every day to be prepared for her humor on a spiritual level. For this reason, a nurtured humor is bold enough to take over a conversation while you enjoy a yellow joke. Equally important, if a woman doesn't know the value of a rose or flower, she doesn't know the value of herself and the giver. Because a rose or flower symbolizes a true woman in essence, a woman is either a lost rose or a found rose.

A Monkey on a Donkey

Have you ever thought about the kind of animal you would look like if you were not a human being? Which animal would you like your spouse to act like? What humor would come out of an entertainment between a monkey and a donkey? A monkey on a donkey. Monkies have a sense of humor. You can see it when they smile naturally. Maybe a monkey can teach a donkey how to live with a nurtured humor.

3. Good Humor Maintains Your Composure

"If the effect of your humor has not made a positive impact on your community, your sense of humor is not ready to make history."

"The way a nurtured humor blossoms prepares your life for what is awesome."

"Pink makes me think. I love pink. It smells goods, tastes good, looks good, and sounds good. If you do not like pink, learn to love it and make it your friend. It can help you think. It is a thought-provoking color. Think with the color of pink."

"A beautiful sense of humor can shine through a dark room."

Chapter 3
The Beauty of Humor

First Impression of a Nurtured Humor

When you stare at the sun, rainbow and clouds and sky, what comes to mind? Preparing yourself to nurture your humor is like removing a brain tumor. The beauty of humor is when faithfulness and righteousness kiss each other.

What color does a nurtured humor have? Why does the sun leave with an orangelike color? What's the first thing most people look for in your character? Most people look to see if your sense of humor can have something in common with their humor. If you wanted to make friends with someone who can help nurture you, would your humor make a positive impact in ten seconds or less?

The way you behave and talk around people lets anyone know what kind of person you are. You would want to have a good first impression because people may consider it your last impression even if it was influenced by a false impression.

The power of a nurtured humor encompasses your heart, mind, body and soul. You don't have to have the best sense of humor in the world. You just need to nurture it, and then it will bring out the best of you. Thinking and feeling with your sense of humor is an awesome way to be ready to serve humanity. For example, a nurtured humor connects you to all kinds of people. Constantly nurturing your sense of humor is a great tool for sharpening yourself and the humor of others.

Positive Stress vs. Negative Stress

Positive stress is optimistic; whereas, negative stress is pessimistic. Even today, some or many people don't know about positive stress because the word 'stress' has a negative connation. There are two kinds of stress. One is positive, and the other one is negative. For example, graduating from high school or college creates positive stress because you are excited and encouraged while you embrace the moment of success. In contrast, depression creates negative stress. Only positive stress can nurture your humor because it knows how to exhilarate, and it keeps the mind of your humor receptive. In addition, positive stress lowers your stress level, yet negative stress increase your stress level. Since negative stress does not nurture your humor, positive stress appreciates your humor while negative stress depreciates your humor.

Silverman Performs a Humorous Machine

Who is silverman? Silverman is a robotic-looking man painted gray from head to toe. His character role is to act like a humorous machine that injects humor in the audience. At the end of the show, everyone is pleased with his humorous performance because he entertains people.

An Institution for Humor

What really makes up an institution? Good humor can bring people together. Your demeanor should always represent the face of your humor. Once people see a sincere smile on your face, it can bring a team of people together. Kindness and gentleness can help build up a team of good humor. Two different kinds of people with a nurtured humor can reconcile a broken friendship or relationship between them. We live in the same planet. Have you self-fulfilled the prophecy of your humor?

Prestige Value of Good Humor

In my Business Law 2 class, I asked my professor, "Is it discrimination if an employer hires a graduate student from a more prestigious university over a graduate student from a less prestigious university?" He said that it would not be discrimination because an employer has the right to make hiring decisions. However, if you nurture your humor enough that the interviewer can see the potential of your excellent work performance, you have a better chance of working for the company. For this reason, pay more attention to the prestige value of your good humor rather than the prestige value of an institution. Besides, students and scholars are the ones who make up the institution not the buildings on campus. If colleges and universities never had an academic purpose for students and scholars, it would not be an institution today.

Good Humor Nurtures Your Self-Esteem

The value of good humor nourishes your self-esteem. There should be a relationship between good humor and your self-esteem. Whatever you value is a reflection of who you are regardless of who you want to become. I value spiritual wisdom, sincere respect and a nurtured humor. These three values can help build your humor to its maximum potential. Your self-esteem cannot prevail without a nurtured humor. Good humor develops and sharpens a beautiful sense of humor.

Good Humor Denies Hatred

Did you ever have one of the worst life experiences that either crippled you or helped bring out the best of you?

If you ever hated anyone, you can utilize any humorous experience to not hate anymore. Hatred takes away your good humor, and it can destroy or shipwreck the faith of your humor. Real love promotes good humor at its best, yet hatred will never make good humor beautiful.

Who's the Black Cat?

In 1997, I was watching an interview on Alonzo Mourning. While the discussion was about the Chicago Bulls, Mourning said that Michael Jordan is like a black cat in terms of agility. As he said that, a scene came in that showed Michael Jordan dunking the ball as if it was a black cat on the court.

4. Good Humor Connects People Together

"A nurtured humor looks wise and beautiful in the eyes of people."

"Even a monkey laughs and smiles for the fun of it."

"A sense of humor that has been nurtured is an important reason for every season."

"Find the proper inspiration with the right motivation for your aspirations."

Chapter 4
Humor is Encouraging

The Encouragement Triangle

Proper Inspiration   **Right Motivation**

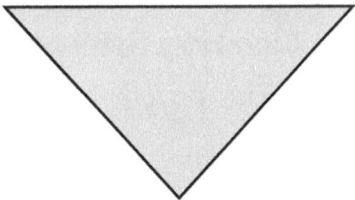

Right Vision for Your Aspirations

Proper Inspiration + Right Motivation =
Right Vision for Your Aspirations

Are You Encouraged Today?

I am very encouraged to see the positive energy of my humor is still growing each and every day.

A person may feel inspired but not motivated until the inspiration finds the right motivation to envision a purpose for the aspirations. When someone or something inspires you, the inspiration needs to carry the right motivation. To keep your heart properly inspired and motivated, it needs a vision to hold the proper inspiration with the right motivation for your aspirations.

For example, if you ever understood what the trinity really means, you would understand the roles in the encouragement triangle (on the previous page). In the trinity, you will learn about the Father, who is God, the Son, who is Jesus Christ and the Holy Spirit, which is the spiritual counselor. Likewise, in the encouragement triangle, the vision has the role of the Holy Spirit because it gives you a sense of prophecy. The proper inspiration has the role of the Father because God inspired the creation of human beings. The right motivation has the role of the Son because Jesus is the right motivation for Christianity. It makes sense to understand the encouragement triangle when you compare it to the character roles in the trinity because it helps you understand the exact nature, mechanism and dynamics of each role in the encouragement triangle. Then, you will see the beauty of encouragement and how it can nurture your humor. Think of it this way, if every planet had a way to link to each other, we would have more resources for survival. In addition, with the proper inspiration with the right motivation, you can learn how to develop your aspirations. You need to work the muscles of the proper inspiration to build new muscles of the right motivation to have spiritual muscles for your aspirations. Today, allow the strength of your humor to encourage someone else's humor.

Humor Brings Out the Best

How do you become better than yourself? It is very encouraging to see how nurturing my humor can bring out the best out of me. I even learned good humor can enhance your work performance in the workplace. For instance, even if you may refuse to apply the code of ethics in the workplace, maintaining good humor can nurture the nature of your heart to learn how to accept the importance of ethics in and out of the workplace. Later on, the application of good humor will prove your heart will want to have a desire for ethics in and out of the workplace. In addition, whether you are at home or in the workplace, do not mistaken good humor for flirtatious jokes or practical jokes. Good humor can bring the best out of you.

The Gift of Encouragement

Encouragement is nourishment. In the body of Christ, the church, I learned my gift is to encourage people for the love of encouragement. Whenever I encourage the heart of someone with a trophy and encouraging letter, it makes me feel encouraged as if that person encouraged me with the gift of encouragement. This is the power of encouragement. Even though I don't expect to receive anything in return, my heart is refreshed whenever I refresh others, and it nurtures my humor. This is part of the beauty of humor. It looks and feels beautiful inside of my heart. I feel encourage to show my sincere appreciation and smile through my nurtured humor that connects with people. As a result, humor meets humor. It's another way to renew your faith and your heart. It keeps your flesh in great shape to stay fresh and encouraged. Nurturing my humor has shown me my greatness and brought out the best I can be. I will let my nurtured humor get the best of me because I have a burning desire to nurture my humor. Most of all, good humor helps improve my attitude, feelings and habits. It promotes positive feelings and a healthy attitude that can build bridges not walls. Good humor will never disown you. Ever since I nurtured my humor, it stabilizes my mood and tranquilizes my mind, heart and soul. Have your humor work for you? Nurturing your humor leaves room for improvement. Be better than yourself.

Write an Encouraging Letter

Encourage someone you know with an encouraging letter. Whenever I would write an encouraging letter to give someone, I find it nurturing my humor. Since life can be harder than it is, we all need the right encouragement because the heart can be hardened by any kind of discouragement. Without the proper inspiration with the right motivation, you will lose the value of the vision for your humor to encourage others. However, to make your life easier and comfortable, you will need the proper inspiration with the right motivation that can give you the right vision for your humor to encourage others and yourself. The proper inspiration with the right motivation is part of nurturing your humor. After you have won the victory over your struggles, your nurtured humor will give you a chance to triumph.

Honor Your Good Humor

A self-rewarding honor nurtures your humor. Although I want you to nurture your humor, you need to be in the mood for good humor because having a mood of good humor will not let your emotions get the best of you. Even though you may not be in a good mood for humor, a mood of good humor can prepare you for any challenges that come your way. You can serve others with your honored good humor.

When I saw how encouraging my mood of good humor can be, I felt compelled to let it shine on other people. Now, I can't imagine life without a mood of good humor. Every day when I wake up in the morning, I am driven by a mood of good humor. A mood of good humor moves me and takes me to newer heights. Also, it expands my walls and horizons. The more I encourage people the more courage I have to grasp the power of encouragement. At the end of my life, I want to be remembered for my generous good humor for others to follow the great examples of my nurtured humor. Good humor wants to accept your life. What do you want to be remembered for? Wouldn't you want students and scholars to be name in your honor of good humor? and How will history remember you?

Humor Serve the Poor and Needy

I like to volunteer my generous time to serve the poor and needy. They say that time is money. Time is money only in a business sense. How much money can buy time? Since money cannot buy the amount of a lifetime, your humor is worth more than time. If you don't have time to serve the poor and needy, find a way to make time to serve them. Back when my grandmother would cook for me, I never took the time to learn how to cook. Since that time, I sought other ways to serve the poor and needy with my gift of encouragement. Furthermore, I served by volunteering my time to get things done for the poor and needy. Finding other ways to serve the poor and needy is a life skill that can help save many lives. In regards to time management, I know a brother in the church who used to never have time to wash his clothes because of his work schedule. When he saw his time was very limited, he would wash his clothes two o'clock in the morning. This is a perfect example of how to manage your time throughout the day. It taught me how to be committed to time management. Just always remember, you can always find time either during the day or at night to do any personal errands that needs to be done on time. When you learn to enjoy the struggles of life, you have found one of the ways to nurture your humor. Time management really works efficiently and effectively.

Surrealism Makes Me Laugh

What can we all have in common? Your common sense would tell you a nurtured humor. If you wake up in the morning and thought it was Monday when it's really Sunday, your humor should be able to laugh and smile with joy. If it has ever happen to you, it will be a humorous mistake.

Even if you don't have a childlike humility, nurturing the spirit of your humor can develop a childlike humility. Also, nurturing your humor can uncover the truth and you can succeed even better. A nurtured humor is your trophy for your life. People who don't think this way are creating a brain tumor for their humor.

Whatever Happen to Punky Booster?

The last time I watched the episode of punky booster was in the early 1990s. Whenever I would watch it, I remember a young girl climbing a tree house where her room was located. Back in those days, the idea of a tree house crossed my mind. Just thinking about the episodes brings back funny memories that will last forever in my mind. I think the episodes should be brought back because it has humorous appeals. While I continue to live my life, I still cherish the punky booster days. Let me now tell you a funny joke. What does punky booster mean to me? To boost the mind of a punky from becoming a junky.

What is Your Favorite Cartoon?

My favorite cartoon has always been woody wood pecker. Termites are known to be a threat to households throughout the communities. What do woody wood pecker and termites have in common? Both of them like to eat wood. However, the funniness that comes out of woody wood pecker is it creates chairs or tables out of wood. I encourage you to reminisce on your favorite humorous cartoons that you can pass on to your offspring. Whether it's a talking bubble gum, Roger Rabbit, Alvin and the Chipmunks, Garfield or Donald Duck, your favorite cartoon can keep you attuned from midnight to afternoon.

Wheelchair Memory Lane

One day at my aunt's house, my sister showed me a funny cartoon clip on the internet. It showed how my brother and I will probably be together in the future. It made sense for my sense of humor. Life is a funny place to be in, and you may not even know it. Even for someone in a wheelchair, good humor can enlighten his or her day. Turn the light bulb of your humor on and never turn it off. Create humorous memories that can take you back on a fun journey. The destiny of good humor is life on earth.

5. Learn to Appreciate and Reciprocate Your Humor

"Never limit your sense of humor because of disappointments, disagreements, discouragements, embarrassments, and frustrations."

"If you don't nurture your sense of humor, it can cost you your life."

"Words of a nurtured humor can paint a picture of a good day."

"Do you find pleasure and satisfaction in your sense of humor?"

Chapter 5
Appreciate and
Reciprocate Your Humor

Pursue the Humor of Joy
and True Happiness

Double your happiness by appreciating and reciprocating your humor whenever you enjoy life to the full. If you enjoy happy hour when you have a chance to meet new people and make new friends, you should help nurture their humor.

When I pursued the humor of joy and true happiness, I had to learn a sincere smile allows me to meet people because it shows them a friendliness about my character. Although this chapter is very short, the pursuit of joy and true happiness can help you find peace for your life. You want your persona and demeanor to match with the spirit of your humor. After you thread humor at human connections into your inner nature, you will have enough humorous jokes for true happy times and for a happy home.

Humor Promotes Social Freedom

In the past, the reason why I was unhappy with my life is because I did not allow my sense of humor to fit my lifestyle. Telling a joke can be funny, but what good is laughing and smiling momentarily if you don't allow humor to fit your lifestyle. Humor is supposed to shine on others when you talk, when you walk, and when you are behind closed doors.

Even if you had a very bad day, keeping humor in mind can enlighten and illuminate your sense of humor. Except for when you have a death in your family, there is no excuse for not nurturing your humor. I learned when humor is part of your life it nurtures you along the way. That is, while you nurture your humor, it is developing humility to rebuild your character. How does this work? If you can recall back to the introduction, you will begin to understand and see how my painful experiences crippled my sense of humor.

However, a pleasant experience can nourish and enrich your humor to behave like a humble child. At the end of the day, despite a bad day, you still want to remind yourself about how nurturing it is to possess a sense of humor. It is a positive-going energy that makes you feel alive each and every single day. Last but not least, good humor promotes social freedom and peace among every culture. Good humor should be part of every culture to see the diversity of humor.

Living with humor improved my social life and spiritual life. Whenever I'm hanging out with friends, we have one thing in common: a sense of humor to share with one another. Once one of my friends laughs while something funny is said, we all enjoy the pleasure of the statement. As a result, living with humor promotes social freedom. Humor can be found from the least important moments to the most important moments. At least I think it does for the most part. It should taste like syrup with fluffy pancakes.

In order for comedians to share funny stories or jokes, the nature and character of their humor must be fully developed and nurtured in their mind, heart and soul.

Protect the Boundaries of Your Humor

Having a sense of humor is one of the building blocks for building a friendship into a relationship.

When I used to have a too serious personality, it would not help people draw closer to me. Even in what you have a passion for, your humor should be able to always stay active throughout the whole time. Protecting the boundaries of your humor also protects your loved ones, relationships and friendships. Since it worked for me, it can definitely work for you. Better yet, living with a good humor teaches me to act the right way. For example, there used to be times when I didn't know how to act and say the right words. After I learned the purpose of nurturing the spirit of my humor, I gained the power of humor. To inject humor in people is a very good starting point and turning point at any given moment. Besides, humor is what you make it. The way you treat your humor is how your humor will treat you. Throughout the whole day, I want my life to be filled with a powerful good humor for the spirit of other people.

Who is Your Role Model?

If you have a role model, does your role model have a nurtured humor? and Does your role model allow his or her humor to play a significant role in his or her life?

Back in my high school days, my old role model did not have a nurtured humor because of all the dramatic events he experienced. Even when he had and showed a bit of humor in his songs, his thug mentality would not allow his humor to breathe properly. His humor came from an improper inspiration with the wrong motivation.

Humor Is Encouraging, one of the chapters in this book, teaches you the encouragement triangle. According to the encouragement triangle, you will learn you must have the proper inspirations with the right motivations for your aspirations.

On the other hand, ever since my college days, I have fallen in love with Lecrae (Christian Hip Hop recording artists), Oprah Winfrey and Les Brown. These three individuals will forever be my role models because they have the proper inspiration with the right motivation to help serve humanity's vision. Oprah Winfrey is like a mother to me while Les brown is like a father to me. I even wrote a poem called 'My Gift to Oprah'. When I studied their roles, their nurtured humor grabbed my attention. You can even see the power and beauty in their humor when they give a life-changing lesson. They speak with charisma, which is part of being an inspirational and motivational speaker and leader. Without charisma, you lose the value of leadership. I have followed the foot steps of Lecrae, Oprah Winfrey and Les Brown. Therefore, it is very important to have a role model who has a nurtured humor that can help nurture the spirit of your humor. It will produce characteristics of a childlike humility. Let the proper inspiration with the right motivation digest in your humor to have the right vision for your aspirations.

Humor and Intellect Go Hand in Hand

Economics is a social science that is usually viewed as a business major probably because business students are required to take it. However, I used to hate economics because I did not nurture my humor to understand the benefits of learning it even though the textbook lacked clarity. At the university level, the textbook was easy to understand because it clarified the points and examples in each chapter. Just like mathematics is a language, I had to understand the language of economics. Once I understood the language of economics, my humor took my intelligence to a higher level. The study of economics became fun and encouraging to my humor. If I had to start my college life all over again, I would start nurturing my humor and create successful jokes regarding the study of economics. As a result, I successfully passed economics with the help of my humor.

Humor Heals Your Speech Impediment

Ever since my pre-teen years, I have been a stutterer. When I studied the fundamentals of speech communication, I learned people who stutter needs to learn how to make humor fit his or her lifestyle. In fact, the more I nurture my humor the less I stutter.

I remember one of my former college friends who told me that he stutters. He told me that when he would practice the pronunciation of words and sentences he would laugh at himself whenever he stuttered. This helped me see laughing at yourself can improve your sense of humor. Even though I've had a very rough life, I've found my touch with my humor by nurturing it.

Character of Integrity Invites Your Humor

When I would take a look at an individual's face that looks nurtured, I used to think that person must have been nurtured. In reality, a nurtured-looking face does not mean a person has been nurtured. Remember the human face comes in different shapes and forms.

It's about finding powerful ways to build the character of integrity in your life for your humor to be nurtured. For example, many people still believe true beauty comes from the outward appearance. It's true that people can look beautiful when you take a closer look at their face. However, true beauty comes from building the character of integrity in your life. When the integrity of your character is developed and nurtured, it can also look beautiful through a smile or laugh. It doesn't hurt to smile or laugh, but your humor needs to be connected with building a character of integrity in your life. Besides, just like anyone can be honest for the wrong reason, you may laugh and smile for the wrong reason due to the wrong ways of building your character. You would not want to laugh and smile for the wrong reason because it serves no purpose. Nurturing your humor teaches you to laugh and smile for the right reason, and it serves the purpose of your life. Then, you will have a smile that will never fade away. Please keep in mind someone who works for only the money has a low integrity in his or her character.

The reason why beauty on the outward appearance fades is because it was never true beauty. Remember what I said earlier, "True beauty comes from building the character of integrity in your life." Hence, once you've built the character of integrity in your life, you will start to see in your body language the beauty and power of a nurtured humor.

Humor Takes On Your Environment

In reality, if the friendships and relationships you have do not nurture other friendships and relationships of yours, you will need to examine the environment where all of these friendships and relationships tend to be in. This is a great indicator because it determines how long these friendships and relationships will last in the future. If there is a chance to develop and nurture the boundaries of your humor, you should let your humor take over. Like when the sun shines on the earth, your sense of humor needs to shine in all of your friendships and relationships from the general ones to the specific ones.

What Are Your Values?

Depending on the culture you live and the things you treasure and value, you need to find the moral values from each of these to nurture your humor. If you don't find them nurturing your humor, I highly recommend you rebuild your culture and learn to cultivate moral values that can nurture your humor for the rest of your life. Overall, your core values, moral values, social values and spiritual values should all be centered around the spirit of your humor.

Good Humor Maintains Childlike Humility

My humor was folded in half until I dismantled my ego. In my past, there was a time when I had no idea of what humility meant. In fact, I never knew a humble smile comes from a nurtured humor. In the heat of any moment, a nurtured humor can rescue you from any potential dangers.

Reward Your Humor

One of the funniest things I thought about doing is giving myself a trophy for how ambitious I am. I learned when you reward yourself you will perform better than you would have if you chose not to reward yourself. Find ways to reward your humor. I already started on mine.

6. Embody
Your Humor

"Life is nothing more than a whip cream on a chicken wing."

"I used to have a serious humor until I nurtured my humor."

"When you nurture your sense of humor, it will develop a mood of humor."

"The way you laugh and smile is just as important as nurturing your humor."

Chapter 6
Humor Makes Me Feel Alive

Humor is Still Alive

Do you feel alive today like you did when you were first born? Do you feel alive when you find good humor out of good memories? How invigorating is it to see and know a nurtured humor has on life?

Although life comes in different shapes and forms, we can still feel the same human blood in our flesh. Nurturing your humor keeps your flesh fresh and brings out the best of you. I had to exemplify the lifestyle of a nurtured humor to know how to embody good humor. In return, It has molded my nature to become a civilized person retroactively. It gave me a young and healthy spirit. I've allowed my nurtured humor to work for me even when times are tough. Not nurturing your humor amounts to nothing.

Too Sensitive Cannot Fit in Good Humor

Nurturing your humor trains your sensitivity to stay in balance, but it doesn't make your sensitivity less sensitive or more sensitive.

Most of my experiences in the past were not pleasant for my humor. When I was a child growing up, my spirit was crushed by many beatings that came my way. Most of the time, I was vulnerable to any insensitive person, and it made me too sensitive as I got older.

Because of these experiences, it molded my sensitivity to feel too sensitive and folded my humor in half until I rebuilt it. I later learned being too sensitive cannot fit in good humor. Just like being too serious with people is not appropriate, being too sensitive takes away your humor and leaves you empty and powerless. On the other hand, enough sensitivity fits in good humor because it gives your humor room to breathe. Like too much of anything is never healthy, too much sensitivity is unhealthy. Today, through the eyes of a new born baby, I can look back and still carry my sense of humor. At the same time, I do notice people who are insensitive usually never carry their sense of humor. No one should be insensitive or too sensitive, but you need enough sensitivity to have a sympathetic understanding for the humor of others. However, there will be rough times that might embitter you. As long as you prepare your sense of humor, you should be able to overcome disappointments, disagreements, discouragements, frustrations and embarrassments. Just like a new born baby has a tender smile, your smile should still stay tender after nurturing the spirit of your humor.

It is very important to be compassionate and considerate toward anyone you meet. Just remember, no one is a robot, and no one should be treated like a robot because we all have sensitive feelings somewhere in our heart. Treat people with sincere respect and you will be treated with the same measure of sincere respect. Why would you want to take away your humor?

Good Humor Has Social Skills

Does good humor allow us to explore what makes us human beings? Being able to socialize with anyone allows you to adapt to the social environment. You can enjoy the company of others in a social environment when you offer a pleasant experience. In addition, anywhere I go to meet new people and people I know, I become a reflection of the social environment even in the workplace environment. When you nurture your humor, your social life, professional life and spiritual life will function even better as a whole to help maintain your new self. The positive energy and rhythm of good humor carries the conversation. The faith of good humor can rest in every area of your life and be the medicine for your soul. Therefore, as long as you know how to socialize effectively, people will keep you in company and agree to a social relationship.

Promote Your New Self

If people view you from a worldly perspective, it is not a good idea to be around them. A worldly perspective will not help people understand your true identity. On the other hand, when I studied Acting 1, I learned the power of acting helps you find who you are and identify your new self. In this dark and evil world, many people still do not know who they are. Some people are a reflection of the nature and mechanism of someone's life while others are lost in space not in touch with reality. If you put yourself in someone's shoe to relate to that person, you need to make sure it doesn't have a negative effect on your life or else other people will not even know the real problem behind your true personality. On the other hand, good humor can help you find who you really are and identify your new self. Take a spiritual approach and become a reflection of good humor, then the nature, mechanism and dynamics of good humor will come sooner. Promote your new self and stay in good health. Have you already identified who you are in reality?

7. Humor Looks For Spiritual Wisdom

"A man who thinks he is God fools only himself and will perish. A man can only be a man of God. Besides, God can never perish, but any man can perish."

"An intellectual clown is someone who uses intelligence as a costume gown."

"Not nurturing your humor is like feeding your flesh and spirit with poison."

"I rather live a short life filled with joy and true happiness than live a long life filled with misery and pain."

Chapter 7
Spiritual Wisdom Has a Humor

What is Spiritual Wisdom?

My definition of spiritual wisdom is to look and clearly understand life the way God looks and understands life in general. Take the story of Adam and Eve as an example. God already knew Adam and Eve would sin before they did sin. So why would the Almighty God, who is sinless, allow sin to be permissible? Without sin, Adam and Eve would not need God's help because they would've been sinless just like God. Unlike conventional wisdom, the fact of the matter is we need God's help on a daily basis. With the help of spiritual wisdom, your humor takes life on a new meaning."

CPR for your Humor

In another book I read a true story about a CPR instructor trying to resuscitate an old man. As he pumped on his chest to move the man's blood, another man stood by and watched. After the CPR instructor gave mouth-to-mouth resuscitation to push fresh air into his lungs, the bystander told the CPR instructor to give up after several minutes the man was still not responding nor was the ambulance arriving. Then, the CPR instructor began to tire physically but continue working hard for several more minutes and had to block out the negative comments which the bystander was making about how the victim was already dead. Finally, the old man coughed, began to breathe for himself, and his pulse returned. The old man was actually conscious and alert by the time the ambulance arrived. Although the old man might've not felt the sensation of the performance by the CPR instructor, the next day in the hospital the CPR instructor learned the old man heard everything that was said while he was knocked unconscious.

In comparison, take the story of Adam and Eve as a great example. Before God created Eve out of Adam, God breathed into Adam's nose the breath of life and then Adam had life. From this great example in the Holy Bible, the true story about the CPR instructor trying to resuscitate an old man is what God did to Adam. In this biblical story, God is the CPR instructor while Adam is the old man who needs God's help on a daily basis and because sin continues to knock Adam unconscious. Like the way God gave Adam mouth-to-mouth resuscitation to push fresh air into Adam's lungs as implied in the biblical scriptures.

This is enough evidence to help you see and clearly understand God always existed. No one can see God because God is invisible. If you could see God, you would have a blind faith that has no purpose to believe in God, and it would defeat the purpose of faith.

When you lose your car keys, don't you have hope you will find it soon or later? Likewise, while you live on earth, you continue to hope to see God in heaven. Anything that is already seen doesn't need your hope because you already can see the physical form. Please keep in mind God doesn't have a physical form. While God is still invisible, God works through men to help you see how powerful he is through human beings. In fact, God is more powerful than you think he is. God could've chosen not to create Adam and Eve and just leave the earth empty.

Having hope in God is part of having faith in Jesus Christ. That is why it is very important to trust God's people who are godly and trustworthy because this is essential to Christianity. Equally important, you will have to live the life of Jesus Christ to clearly understand the exact nature, mechanism and dynamics of Christianity because Christianity is very compelling. Also, if you want to be spiritually enlightened, the life of Christ is a very great way to start your journey.

I know for sure nurturing the spirit of your humor is good for your conscious. It feeds your conscious with spiritual vitamins and minerals. For example, most poets are conscious of their inner thoughts and feelings that keep them aware. I know because I am a poetry writer myself. Whenever I write a poem, my inner thoughts and feelings keep me aware of what is right and wrong with the structure of my poems.

Whether you're a songwriter or any kind of writer, your inner thoughts and feelings give you an urge to do right despite your intention. Life is a writer. That is, the way you live your life is the way you draw your belief. So whatever you feed your mind, heart and soul builds up the character you are feeding in your conscious. When the eyes of your heart are open, this is when you know you are spiritually awake.

If there was a way to diagnose the essence of your humor, what would it reveal about your character?

Better yet, what would the diagnosis of the global economy reveal about the world's humor as a whole? Would it be good humor or bad humor?

What would be the symptoms of the global economy's humor for the future generations?

In addition, just like no one has ever seen God, no has ever seen how the wind looks like when it is felted. Could the wind be another representation of God?

The answer to this wise question can be answered through the insights of spiritual wisdom.

Sarcasm Degrades Your Humor

Based on my observations, I notice the exact nature of sarcasm is very deceptive and pessimistic. It has no foundation and no purpose to help nurture your humor. In fact, it leaves you with the wrong impression. The euphemism behind sarcasm is to use mild sarcastic expressions to make you believe sarcasm is healthy for your humor when it really is not. A euphemist cannot properly fit the role of a humorist or comedian and would not be able to nurture your humor because the tone of the expression will still imply a distasteful, offensive and unpleasant mood to the spirit of your humor. Also, it would be treating you as if you're an animal in a cage and degrading the character of your humor. Sarcasm mocks and ridicules your humor.

However, the power of a nurtured humor avoids the nature of sarcasm. Without first nurturing your humor, you will run into a brick wall and not have a humorous impression on others. If after you nurture your humor, your life of good humor can prove sarcasm degrades and dehumanizes the character of your humor, and for anyone who wants to be sarcastic. Please understand sarcasm makes no sense at all. It has no foundation to help build your self-esteem. The fact of the matter is reality collides with dreams and fantasies and generates a sense of conflict within your mind.

Can Artificial Intelligence Promote Good Humor?

My former college friend who did not clearly understand the meaning of artificial intelligence. He thought it was another form of wisdom. How can artificial intelligence be a form of wisdom since it's not part of reality? It's like a human clone without a soul. Also, anything that is artificial is not natural. However, like good humor, spiritual wisdom is a natural lifestyle. For example, back in high school, I used to think the sneakers that Michael Jordan wore in a basketball game are the same sneakers that other students would wear in school. After I learned the difference, I learned Jordan wore the authentic type while the students wore the imitation type of the authentic type.

Also at the time, my former college friend understood the spiritual process of baptism but could not understand the difference between 'what is authentic' and 'what is artificial.' My former college friend really needed to know the difference between 'what is authentic' and 'what is artificial.' While some or most people still think they pay for the authentic type of a pair of sneakers, they are really paying for the name of the shoe or sneaker that they bought. Do you now get the point? Spiritual wisdom is authentic while artificial intelligence is just an imitation of intelligence but is unnatural. The humor of spiritual wisdom continues to laugh at artificial intelligence because it has no foundation. In addition, artificial intelligence can be used as a power of deceit to manipulate the human mind. It attempts to duplicate spiritual wisdom like people who counterfeit money, but it will never be the same. Back when God created Adam and Eve, God never used a machine to create them. Notice how men use machines to clone a human body, but God uses his natural creativity and his spiritual wisdom to create human beings out of him. Equally important, cell phones, computers, and technology-related stuff please the human eye but can blind the eyes of the heart. Nothing is wrong with technology yet too much of it is not healthy for your soul. If you worship technology, it becomes a trapping. Technology cannot bear spiritual wisdom.

As a result, artificial intelligence cannot promote good humor because it is a form of ignorance. Besides, spiritual wisdom is the absence of artificial intelligence. Can artificial intelligence bear spiritual wisdom? It can never bear spiritual wisdom.

Are the Eyes of Your Conscious Open?

In my introduction to psychology class, my psychology professor asked the class, "How do you know when your conscious is awake?

No one in the classroom answered the question until I said, "When the eyes of your conscious are open."

You may be intellectually awake, politically awake or even mentally awake but may not be spiritually awake?

On a scale between zero and ten, where would you rate your sense of humor? Is your humor in touch with reality? Does your humor feel at peace with your comfort zone?

Unlike the questions some philosophers would ask, these wise questions are necessary because you need to learn how to maintain awareness at all times. You can learn to keep your conscious spiritually awake by nurturing your humor and to separate your intelligence from your emotions.

Is Your Humor Spiritually Awake?

How would you know when your humor is spiritually awake? When you know the eyes of your heart are open. A person can be intellectually awake, politically awake or mentally awake but may not be spiritually awake. So how do you know when you are spiritually awake?

If you don't understand why you live the way you do and why you do the things you do, you are spiritually blind.

You will need to feed the mind, body and soul of your humor with inner wisdom and with inner peace to have conscious control over your sense of humor.

Now ask yourself these questions, how should my heart feel when my emotions get the best of me? How should my mind think when I start to lose faith? and How should my body adapt to my heart, mind, and soul?

On the other hand, no one can be fully awake due to the imperfection of the human nature. If your conscious was fully awake, you would be perfect. Also, you would not have character flaws. In addition, surrealism is a perfect example of the imperfections of the human nature. There were days when I would wake up in the morning and I thought it was Monday when it really was Sunday. This is an indication of how the conscious can never be fully awake but it can be spiritually awake. On a spiritual level, even though I thought it was Monday when it really was Sunday, I then realize it was Sunday. Therefore, we are conscious of what we are aware of. In this case, my conscious was not aware of Monday morning when I thought it was Sunday.

Do Humans Really Have a Third Eye?

If you ever heard anyone say, "My third eye." Just keep in mind it means the mind's eye. In a spiritual sense, it's funny to know about your mind's eye because it can be expanded to increase your creativity, knowledge and wisdom to produce creative thoughts. It also inspires creativity. For example, whether you believe in God or not, your mind's eye can grasp the existence of the invisible in your mind. Though God is invisible, God can be seen through other people in terms of righteousness. How can this be? Trusting in the power of God through someone can really show you someone else's potential. When I studied the Holy Bible in college, my former mentor saw an inner power in me that I had not seen at the time. In fact, I had to become a true disciple of Jesus in order to know and live my purpose in life. Even at that time, I had to look at life from a spiritual perspective to walk in the road of success. Now ask yourself, "Am I living my true purpose on earth?" There was a time you did not exist and there will be another time you will not exist in the future. Your third eye can help you plant the seeds for survival and set an example for the future generations.

Hypnosis for Your Humor

Have you ever tried hypnosis to enrich your humor? Hypnosis can work to better improve your humor as long as the hypnotist does not manipulate your conscious the wrong way through hypnotism.

Christian Comedy Night

Someone would ask, "What is meant by Christian Comedy Night?" Christian Comedy Night was a creative idea I had for a guy who would share jokes whenever we ran into each other. This creative idea is still floating in the air until someone takes it and uses it to help nurture the spirit of others.

On the other hand, although true Christians are not known to be funny because of their spiritual convictions, there is nothing wrong with creating spiritual-related jokes that can nurture your humor. Just think about how creative and humorous 'Christian Comedy Night' can be for everyone in the world. In fact, you can find humor in certain biblical scriptures. For example, I wrote a poem, *Sin*, which had to do with the characteristics of sin. After I wrote it based on my spiritual mindset, I found a comical element that was spiritual-related but funny enough to make you laugh: **"Sin is a demon. It itches like demons in my semens."** When I shared this with a brother in the church, he and I laughed and could not stop. Until this day, whenever we see each other, we still laugh about this comical element found in my poem. The poem still carries the moral value but is funny enough to make anyone laugh. Now you can see how something spiritual-related can have a comical element for laughter. Besides, humor can be found anywhere as long as you find the humorous insights to share with other people, and good humor is healthy for your spirituality.

Christianity vs. Religion

What is the difference between Christianity and religion? I first need you to understand learning and studying religion at a nonreligious-based university is totally different from learning and studying it a nonreligious-based university. For instance, if you take a theology class at a non religious-based university, you will not learn the Christianity view because the foundation is base on a worldly perspective unless the instructor is a true disciple of Jesus Christ. Keep in mind secular (nonreligious-based universities) is not intended to be sacred. On the contrary, if you take the class at a religious-based university, you will learn the Christianity view, which is essential to understanding discipleship. I don't need a degree in journalism or literature to write this book. My nurtured humorous experiences have embraced spiritual wisdom. Likewise, **that is why real life experiences in Christianity are more important than a university degree in theology. If someone just has a university degree in theology but is not living the**

life of Jesus Christ, what good is it to just know the knowledge of theology without spiritual wisdom? It's meaningless because your life has no meaning. and Why waste the energy of your intelligence that doesn't exemplify the lifestyle of a true Christian?

Additionally, the word 'Christian' can sometimes have a negative connotation because the lifestyle of a religious person differs from the lifestyle of a true disciple of Jesus Christ. Before I go into further details about these two different lifestyles, you need to understand the difference between Christianity and religion. Christianity is a non-denominational church that includes all types of people from different cultural backgrounds; whereas, religion is a denominational religious church that includes certain types of people. If you read James 1 verse 27 in the Holy Bible, it clarifies the kind of religion that God accepts. This means orphans and widows could be anyone from a cultural background.

On the other hand, theology is the study of God. It teaches you the different kinds of religion in the world. Clearly, religion is manmade, but Christianity is Godmade. Also, Christianity is simple and clear to understand the teachings in the Holy Bible and teaches you the facts of life. Not the facts of life in terms of psychology. It is always better to study theology to grasp the meaning of Christianity and live the life of Christ than to study religion.

Studying and learning theology can help you relate to a religious person when you share the gospel and your faith with that individual. Again, living the life of Jesus Christ is more important than a university degree in theology.

True Disciple of Jesus vs. Religious Person

In actuality, the world that we live in considers true disciples of Christ religious even though they are not religious. That is, the word 'religious' is inappropriate for a true disciple of Christ. Although a religious person is a church-going person, it doesn't mean the individual is a true disciple of Jesus. What makes a true disciple of Jesus different from a religious person is the lifestyle behind his or her faith. Unlike a religious person, a true disciple tends to always develop spiritual convictions and work on character-building to become more like Jesus. Unlike a true disciple of Jesus, a religious person tends to still be worldly and does not keep a tight rein on his or her tongue. In other words, a true disciple of Jesus would not sin deliberately, yet you may find a religious person sinning deliberately because of a shallow foundation in his or her character. Now of course someone who is a true disciple of Jesus may fall into sin because that individual is still a human being (sinner). However, as you study the character of a true disciple of Jesus, you will notice that individual overcame his or her sin by the right kind of faith. In order for a religious person to become a true disciple of Jesus, he or she would have to study the Holy Bible with someone who is already a true disciple of Jesus and study discipleship to clearly understand the meaning of a true disciple of Jesus. Equally important, the word 'disciple' comes from the word 'discipline.' Another word for 'disciple' is 'student.' I wouldn't be surprise to learn about a scholar who has a university degree in theology not know the meaning of discipleship because theology studies the linguistics of religion. When I studied the Holy Bible with a group of true disciples of Jesus, I learned someone who is a true Christian is also a true disciple of Jesus because the word 'disciple' is a synonym for the word 'Christian.'

Back to the subject matter, like I said before, real life experiences in Christianity is more important than a university degree in theology. A religious person can become a true disciple of Jesus as long as that person is humble, discipline and repents completely while studying the Holy Bible with a true disciple of Jesus. That's what it took for me to become a true disciple of Jesus.

Scholar vs. Student

Even though a student and a scholar have similarities, they are not the same. A student tends to be a follower instead of becoming a student leader. However, even though a scholar is also a student, a scholar tends to be a student leader after following great examples of another leader. Leadership is very important because without it you can be misled by any influential leader who makes serious mistakes. By becoming a scholar, you can also become a great leader. A student can become a scholar if he or she chooses to adapt to the lifestyle of a scholar. Equally important, it may take any student years to become a scholar because of lack of preparation outside of class. Overall, even though a student and a scholar have similar roles, a student tends to be a follower while a scholar tends to be a student leader.

Humorous Wisdom

What do spiritual wisdom and good humor have in common?

Wisdom stands for wise, insight, sensible, discernment, oracle and guess what the last letter stands for? Maturity. If you can add up the meaning of these words together, you will begin to understand the meaning of spiritual wisdom. A sense of humor is not necessarily a sign of intelligence. Keep in mind too much intelligence is dangerous because intelligence alone is robotic in your mind. Here are some words of wisdom: "Your sense of humor doesn't need to be competitive to have humorous wisdom."

Does Logic Always Work?

Humor laughs at logic because logic doesn't always work in real life. For example, have you ever thought about how modern day philosophers (lawyers) cannot take logic beyond their intelligence? Why is that so? Let me explain. You must clearly understand logic is 100% but doesn't always apply to real life situations. For example, an atheist believes a car has a creator but does not believe the earth and universe also has a creator (God). This is a paradox, an irrational belief, because the atheist is not using analogies to understand the relationship between the creation and the creator (God). You can feel the wind outside but cannot see its existence. Also, it is absurd to try to use logic since spiritual wisdom is beyond logic. It is absurd to believe the creation of a car has a creator but not believe the creation of the earth has a creator (God). Although spiritual wisdom is logical, it goes beyond logic to stay in touch with reality.

As a result, logic alone is not enough to grasp every thing in reality. Logic based on theory is an approximation of reality, and therefore it can be absurd to use logic base on the human perspective instead of the spiritual perspective.

The Failure of Philosophy

Reality cannot be changed. Philosophers should have included spiritual wisdom in their search for the truth and in their thinking process when they were seeking wisdom.

In philosophy, I learned to seek wisdom but found only bits of it. In reality, you have the ability to seek and find wisdom as long as you are seeking wisdom with the right motive.

However, because most philosophers were seeking their own way of finding wisdom, they fail to plan and plan to fail.

In addition, philosophers should have included God, who is the true father of wisdom, in their search for the truth and in their thinking process because it would've given them a sense of spiritual wisdom.

Equally important, true wisdom is shown through true humility. In fact, wisdom and humility go hand in hand. A nurtured humor sustains humility. Did philosophers have a nurtured humor?

Most philosophers were not humble enough to allow God to give them spiritual wisdom generously. When I studied philosophy in college, I could not believe at how most philosophers would not look for spiritual wisdom through true humility that would've led them to God, who is the true father of wisdom and of humility. At this point, I am confident you now understand the difference between 'seeking wisdom' and 'knowing wisdom.'

Philosophy cannot be justified or be combined with the truth of reality because it would give you a distorted view on life. Another problem with philosophy is it constantly asks unnecessary questions that have nothing to do with the nature of spiritual wisdom. Please keep in mind I really enjoyed studying philosophy but you must still keep reality in perspective on all subject matters because you don't want to be deceived and be misled to believe something that does not coincide with reality. Most of the lessons I learned in class were based on theory and could not be verified. Philosophy does not have a solid foundation. It is manmade and is still seeking wisdom until this day. Just keep this mind, philosophers did not create the heaven and earth in seven days.

Does Water Really Equal H_2O?

As you may already know, in the courtroom, if you cannot prove your argument, you will lose the case.

When I had taken 'Critical Thinking/Ethics in the Workplace,' a course taught in college, my professor told the class, "Water equals H_2O has never been proven before." It's funny because college and university students are taught to believe in this theory.

He then asked the class, "Can you prove water equals H_2O?"

No one could prove it because it's just an approximation of reality. You see, when a concept has never been proven before and continues to stay the same, it is meaningless to try to argue your point against the truth of the matter even if it's part of your field of study. Also, you cannot validate a concept that has never been proven before. The fact of the matter is water equals H_2O is an approximation of reality. In other words, it comes close to reality but still cannot be proven.

Unlike the Maslow's theory, the theory of water is equal to H_2O cannot be justified. Also, it has no realistic value. That is, unrealistic theories disregard the real truth about any subject matter. On the other hand, even though Maslow's theory is still a theory, at least it has realistic values that are relevant to life in general. You need to ask yourself, **"Can this theory be put into practice?"** If it cannot be put into practice, it is a problem to reality. What is the nature of the theory? Does it have a realistic mechanism? and Can the dynamics explain the reasons for the process of the realistic mechanism? It's like a criminal lawyer who wants to practice civil law but has no experience in civil law. A lawyer that does this sets himself up for failure. The fact of the matter is even if you hire the most expensive lawyer to try to prove water is equal to H_2O will be a waste of time for you and your lawyer. Water equals H_2O is a myth.

On the other hand, though Maslow's theory is also theoretical, at least you can relate to this kind of theory because it provides realistic values for human life. For instance, when you study and learn the hierarchy of Maslow's theory, you will understand the most important needs for survival is found at the bottom of the pyramid. Between the foundation and the top of the pyramid, you also learn other important needs for survival and for success. Think of it as a mountain you are walking on, you must start walking from the lowest level to get to the highest level of the mountain. Once you reach the highest level of the mountain, you can see the surroundings of your success. This is how Maslow's theory prepares you for survival at the highest level. This is funny because the hierarchy of Maslow's theory is shaped like a triangle, which is how a mountain looks like in real life.

Now ask yourself, "How does water equal H_2O relate to your life? It really can't relate to life. When you drink water, how important is H_2O to drinking water that can save you from dehydration?

Although certain theories can relate to life, not all theories can relate and be applied to life unless it gives meaning to life like the Maslow's theory. Needless to say, when I applied the Maslow's theory, it's no longer a theory when I take a closer look at how my life was process from birth to where I am today. For some people who are rich, they may not need to follow the highest level of the Maslow's theory because the amount of money they have protects them from certain obstacles that I had to face in my life. When you haven't found success within your reach, it means you need to nurture your humor with the basic needs for survival to succeed in life. In other words, you need the basic needs of life in order to advance to the next level.

Your mind can grow as long as you feed it with profound books and spiritual wisdom. Spiritual wisdom has a great humor to help nurture the spirit of your humor. Nurture the spirit of your humor to last forever.

College Education Helped Nurture My Humor

When I look back at my college days, a college education gave me only educational wisdom. Though some of the knowledge were related to spiritual wisdom, such as psychology and sociology, I had to discern the knowledge of college to better understand the purpose of theories and concepts I learned. I learned most of the knowledge in college is about 90% theory and 10% is based on facts.

College is like a mother and father who can nurture you. After graduating from high school, I lost my sense of humor due to the nature of the high school environment that I was in. However, when I went to college, my college life fulfilled the emptiness in my life that was created by my high school experience. In other words, college nurtured me enough to help me understand a college life should be based on moral values.

On the other hand, there are people who take classes at a college or university just to upgrade a skill that they have. For example, for someone who wants to learn how to write a film script, most colleges and universities offer film writing classes that can teach you how to write a successful film script.

In addition, there are other people who take classes for business purposes. For example, someone who wants to establish a business will need to know the principles of accounting, management and economics because these subject matters coincide with each other to some degree. In fact, if you look to manage your own business, just know a manager must know how to do basic accounting in order to fix any financial errors in the financial statements. Please keep in mind you never want to establish a business before learning how to do basic accounting and know which accounting software to use for your business. While college nurtures you, it disciplines your character unless you're not living a moral life that keeps everything in the right perspective. Indeed, you will not know how valuable a college education is until you live the college life.

If Dogs Could Talk

If dogs knew how to talk, would they tell the truth if they were witnesses to a crime scene or would they lie about the truth?

In the late 1990s, there was a funny commercial that showed a dog laughing at a guy who was sitting on a chair watching television in the living room. While the dog was laughing, the guy looked at the dog and could not believe the dog laughed. The dog laughed so much that the guy was amaze. This is how your humor should be when you are around people who need to be nurtured. This funny commercial was intended to inject humor in television watchers. Without a doubt, it spread humor among television watchers. Just imagine a humorous communication between a dog and a cat. If cats and dogs had spiritual wisdom, they would share humorous wisdom about human beings.

Can You Really Embody White/Black Color?

A nurtured sense of humor would laugh at someone who still thinks people are either white or black. For example, in our society today, most people still use the word 'white' and 'black' to refer to people who are either light skin or dark skin. If you take a closer look at the human skin, no one has the exact color of a white paper or black folder. This is funny because it would be a mismatch that is not even close to reality.

How can anyone embody a color that does not match his or her own skin? Look at how funny it is when most people still can't see the exact color of the human skin. This fallacy has misled many people. On the contrary, the appropriate phrase to use is 'light skin' or 'dark skin' because it clarifies the meaning of the human skin color.

The Makeup of Your Character

Do you know why you live the way you do? What makes up your sense of humor? Whether you know it or not, most people are spiritually blind. They don't know why they do the things they do. For example, back in my younger days, I was influenced to have a thug mentality because my mother chose a neighborhood that seemed to look convenient but was surrounded by a hostile environment. Just like looks can be deceiving, the outward appearance of any neighborhood can fool your eyes.

If I had to choose a place to stay in for my mother, brother, and sister, I would not have chosen the neighborhood I was raised in because the people there did not know how to unify the community.

You should be able to find yourself in the right place in your own community and volunteer to improve the environment surrounding your community. In other words, learn how to police your own community and people will respect your community. Instead, most of the guys who went to the same school as me were living for the street mentality they cultivated. They would live for the wrong pleasure and expect people to sympathize and compromise with their street values that make no sense. They should have separated themselves from their comfort zone to allow themselves to see how precious life can be through a nurtured humor.

When I studied introduction to psychology, I had to learn how to control my environment and not let it control me (locus of control). For example, back in my old neighborhood, most of the people who stayed there did not accomplish anything in life because they allowed the street environment or an irrational belief to take control of them. After I separated myself from these kinds of people, I was able to graduate from high school and went to college to improve my life. I then graduated from college.

I truly think it has a lot to do with the role model you choose to follow. While growing up, I really never had a role model to lead me in the right direction. I used to love one of the greatest rapper of all time. After nearly 10 years, as I studied this rapper, I learned he was not the character who I thought he was. I then understood the makeup of his character, and why he would act the way he did. In fact, I don't think this individual understood himself enough to examine the makeup of his character. Without a doubt, I truly believe if he had a positive role model to look up to, he would have had some wisdom to see his life was headed for the road of self-destruction. Why would someone still walk in the road of self-destruction after reaching the road of international success? That is like standing on top of the roof and landing on your knees after you knew you jumped the wrong way. For instance, if you reach your career destination but your character does not fit the moral values of your duty, it really means you were not meant for that career even though you succeeded. Therefore, we were all meant to live with moral values since no one can thoroughly succeed based on wickedness. Furthermore, if you do reach a certain successful level, you need to be around people who can help nurture your humor because humor takes on the environment. You need to be able to find yourself in the right place at the right time or else you will still be lost in this dark world.

Equally important, bad humor darkens your mind and corrupts your heart and your character because it's intended to degrade your character. On the contrary, good humor is like being around positive people who can nourish and promote your laughter. Besides, optimism promotes good humor for all of us. Therefore, I cannot imagine life without optimism because without it life would be boring and uninteresting. Enjoy yourself when you nurture your humor since you have only one life to live. Live your life to the maximum potential of a good humor. I've already started. So can you.

Spiritual Character of Humor

From a spiritual perspective, good humor plays a spiritual role that is invisible. Right before a sensible joke is made, a nurtured humor waits for the punch line. It takes you back to special memories of your humor. As you learn to nurture the spirit of your humor, even your soul can grasp the spiritual qualities of the spirit of your humor. Hopefully, you can pass some of your nurturing experiences to others who desperately need to nurture the spirit of their humor. The value of nurturing your humor can be attributed to the characteristics of your life. Does your heart beat the vibration of your humor?

Alert vs. Paranoid

What does a skeptical person, cynical person and paranoid person have in common?

I met a guy who served in the military. When he introduced himself to me, I notice the first thing he said was that examining the environment can keep him paranoid. When I heard this, I knew something was wrong with the way he thinks because someone who is paranoid tends to have irrational ways of thinking. When I studied his character, I also learned he is extremely suspicious about the world, and the ideas that are formed in his mind generates and calculates fallacies. He would make me think I am wrong for something that I was totally innocent of. At one time, I learned he was crooked and devious when he lied to me. His paranoid mindset was full of foolishness. Later on, even one of his employees told me that he is nasty in terms of the way he thinks. This guy really needs to renew his mind because his thinking process is very dangerous to any humorous environment. Furthermore, whenever he would shake my hand, he never looked me in the eye. I can imagine what kind of person he is behind close doors.

The truth of the matter is paranoia never keeps you alert. Like sarcasm, it's another way to degrade and corrupt the conscious of your humor. On the other hand, being alert helps nurture your humor because you have a higher chance of finding humor out of things you are aware of. Also, it helps keep your conscious awake and being alert adds to your intelligence. Even any psychologist or therapist would tell you that his way of thinking is abnormal for his mind. Renewing your mind is part of nurturing your humor. Alertness is upgrading you while paranoia is degrading you.

Music Does Penetrate Your Soul

When I used to listen to worldly rap music, it never inspired me to renew my faith, my attitude and my lifestyle. This is one of the reasons why I could not progress in my music career.

Keeping a childlike humility can definitely nurture and grow your sense of humor. Ever since I stopped buying worldly Hip-Hop music and started listening to Christian Hip-Hop, it filtered my mind, heart and soul through humor. It also made me more aware of my potential.

Christian Hip-Hop music promotes and generates positive vibes that has the proper inspiration with the right motivation. Besides that it helps advance the mission of the church, you gain an awareness about worldly Hip-Hop music is another way to poison your flesh and soul.

In fact, kids can grasp the message of a Christian Hip-Hop song because the music is clear and simple to understand. Also, you will never hear profane language or abusive language from a real Christian recording artist. When you listen to it, it also gives you a sense of poise. Christian music has always been clean, spiritual and godly. I truly believe Christian Hip-Hop music is here to rebuild the culture of Hip-Hop that is in the world. Christian Hip-Hop can help save future Hip-Hop recording artists in the next generation from self-destruction. Except for certain secular music that are spiritual-related, most secular music is still missing the spiritual values that Christian Hip-Hop and R&B provides in a song that helps nurture your humor. Christian Hip-Hop music continues to protect the spirit of my humor from worldly music that degrades and corrupts the heart and character of humor. Overall, the kind of music you feed your soul with can either promote or demote your moral character. What kind of music would the spirit of good humor listen to?

True Love Nurtures Good Humor

I notice people who have been nurtured by their parents, who are caring and loving, tend to be less shallow than people who were not nurtured. For example, I wasn't nurtured because my mother did not know how to love me, and my father never wanted to reveal himself to me. The fact of the matter is if you don't know the characteristics of how to love you will not know how to love your own children.

Additionally, you learn the characteristics of true love in the Holy Bible (1 Corinthians 13: 1-13) and then put it into practice and develop it in your character of humor. In other words, you can develop the characteristics of true love to nurture your humor in your character and make it a personality. Besides, even if you were born with true love, you would still need to develop the characteristics of it because you have character flaws that always need to be removed. This goes to show you we will never be perfect in life. Only God, Jesus and holy angels are perfect. If people were perfect, we would not need God's help and have to nurture the spirit of our humor. Also, if people did not make mistakes, we would not know the opposite of perfection.

Godly Fear vs. Worldly Fear

Godly fear is a holy fear that is awesome for your humor. However, worldly fear is an irrational fear that discourages and hinders your humor. Also, worldly fear promotes a tumor for your humor. Have you ever thought about what is the makeup of your fear?

At first, I didn't understand why I need to fear God. I later learned it taught me to live by the right kind of faith and not live under the law. Without thinking twice, a God-fearing man or woman knows how to worship God because his or her fear is based on a biblical foundation. Also, a godly fear teaches you how to stay out of trouble. It is base on a deep respect for the laws. In addition, I truly think another reason why most philosophers did not include God in their thinking and in their search for truth is because they did not have a godly fear. A godly fear can help you understand spiritual wisdom. Why fear men when you need to fear God who is in full control of everything?

Overall, it is very important to clearly understand materialism and technology cannot nurture the spirit of your humor. If you had only one chance to entertain the whole world, how would you present your humor?

Take good care of your humor. Thank you for your generous consideration and time.

Your nurtured humor,

Luckner Pierre

About the Author

After writing a book of poems, Luckner is transitioning into a career as an inspirational writer and screenwriter. Luckner is also a Hip-Hop recording artist.

Luckner earned an AA degree in Accounting. His other books include *Christian Hip Hop Dynasty, A Romantic Spirit: Enjoy Passion for Fashion, CPA Wisdom for Accounting Students, Invisible Anger Meets Domestic Violence, From Boston to Miami: Derek Basketball, She's A Bartender: It's Her Bar Saloon, A Lucky Doll in 3000, Life Demands Respect, The Destiny of Poetry: Life in 3000, Comedy Life Starring Larry Dawg, 100-Yard Field Goal: Who Thought It Could Be Possible?, and Street Wisdom: Let's Take It Back To The 80'S And 90'S*

Nurture the Spirit of Your Humor
Dedicated to nurturing your humor

One day I went to the beach
I stared at the sun rays
as I stared, poetry arrived
in search of me, it came with humor

I felt a sense of serenity with a spiritual remedy
the spirit of humor spoke to me
with patience, poise, pleasure and peace on a spiritual level
a rush of energy gave me confidence

all of a sudden, I wasn't shallow anymore
my spirit became rich even though I am poor
if it wasn't for the faith of humor,
my life would be inside of a brain tumor

materialism or technology cannot nurture your humor
if anyone cannot laugh at all times,
life is not worth living
the destiny of good humor is life on earth

www.ingramcontent.com/pod-product-compliance
Lightning Source LLC
Chambersburg PA
CBHW020302290526
45784CB00003B/1337